CW00959850

Crochet for Beginners

The Step-by-Step Guide Full of Images and Illustration to Learn How to Realize Crochet Patterns You Like

By

Ava Miller

© **Copyright 2021 by Ava Miller - All rights reserved.**

This document is geared towards providing exact and reliable information in regards to the topic and issue covered. The publication is sold with the idea that the publisher is not required to render accounting, officially permitted, or otherwise, qualified services. If advice is necessary, legal or professional, a practiced individual in the profession should be ordered.

From a Declaration of Principles which was accepted and approved equally by a Committee of the American Bar Association and a Committee of Publishers and Associations.

In no way is it legal to reproduce, duplicate, or transmit any part of this document in either electronic means or in printed format. Recording of this publication is strictly prohibited and any storage of this document is not allowed unless with written permission from the publisher.

All rights reserved. The information provided herein is stated to be truthful and consistent, in that any liability, in terms of inattention or otherwise, by any usage or abuse of any policies, processes, or directions contained within is the solitary and utter responsibility of the recipient reader. Under no circumstances will any legal responsibility or blame be held against the publisher for any reparation, damages, or monetary loss due to the information herein, either directly or indirectly.

Respective authors own all copyrights not held by the publisher.

The information herein is offered for informational purposes solely and is universal as such. The presentation of the information is without a contract or any type of guarantee assurance.

The trademarks that are used are without any consent, and the publication of the trademark is without permission or backing by the trademark owner. All trademarks and brands within this book are for clarifying purposes only and are owned by the owners themselves, not affiliated with this document.

Contents

Introduction

Crochet is a technique for making clothing or textiles by interlocking yarn loops with a crochet hook. To put it another way, a hook is used to join yarn to produce something. Crochet may include wire, thread, yarn, or twine, as well as other strand materials. Crochet is originated from a French expression that means "small hook."

Many people mix up the words "crochet" and "knit," believing they are synonymous. Although they are identical, there are several significant variations. For instance, if you present a knitted item to a crochet friend and ask to create one, they might not be capable of doing so. Crochet and knit designs are somewhat different, and it is difficult to convert a knit pattern to a crochet pattern. Knitting generally requires the use of knitting needles (2 in number), which differs from Crochet in the way thread is interlocked. Knitting involves transferring the whole project between the two needles.

Crochet uses just one hook, and instead of moving the material needle to needle, the end product is left on the item itself. Another significant distinction is how Crochet and knit feel to us. A finished knitting swatch can vary from a finished crochet swatch in appearance and feel. Knitting is usually lighter and more compact than crocheting. Crochet consists of knots stacked parallel to each other and on top of each other. The final product is normally less soft than Crochet but more durable.

Although there is a question over which is safer, for beginners, I would prefer crocheting over knitting. There's a good explanation for this: if you make an error in Crochet, it's far simpler to dismantle the project and repair it. It's far more difficult to correct errors while knitting. Even so, most people believe that spinning or crocheting is better for them because of what they knew first. So, if you begin out weaving, Crochet would come more easily to you than knitting and vice versa.

Chapter 1: Fundamentals of Crochet

1.1 Short History

Crochet comes from the French word "crochet," which means "small hook." Crochet's roots, not like needlework and knitting, are difficult to find. Crochet, according to some scholars, emerged in Arabia, spread to Tibet, and then to Spain, where it was adopted Arabian and Mediterranean countries. Other scholars believe Crochet originated in South America, where indigenous peoples were said to wear crocheted ornaments. Finally, there is proof that Crochet began in China, as early crocheted dolls have been discovered. Crochet is thought to have originated from Tabouring, needlework that was a connection between lacework and the crochet work we recognize today. Crochet was a fine approximation of lace and was prevalent in the lower classes since lace was too costly. Crochet first gained popularity in Europe during the early nineteenth century, thanks to Mlle Riego de la Branchardiere's ability to turn needle and lace designs into repeatable crochet patterns. Crochet lacework was adopted as a means of famine relief in the 19th century when Ireland was experiencing the Irish Famine (1845-1849). Crochet provided a source of income for families, allowing them to save enough money to emigrate. Crochet was a favorite of Queen Victoria's, and she also taught herself how to do it!

Crochet is regarded as healing in Denmark, taken in Holland, heckling in Norway, and virkning in Sweden. Throughout the ages, a number of ingredients were used to Crochet, which includes: grasses, hair, reeds, hemp, animal fur, wool, flax, gold, copper, silver strands, silk, white cotton threads, wool yarns. Lingers, morse (walrus tusk), Crochet Tools across the years were: hooks made of metal, fishbone, wood, animal bone, horn, teeth from discarded combs, bronze, mother-of-pearl, old spoons, tortoiseshell, ivory, gold, stone, morse (walrus tusk), vulcanite, silver ebonite, and agate. The very earliest printing of the patterns of crotchet was in the 1840s.

1.2 Materials, Tools, and Supplies

To begin crocheting, you'll need the following materials and supplies:

• Stitch Markers

 • Crochet Hook(s) (optional)

• Hook Case • Yarn (optional, but can be necessary)

• Needle for Tapestry (also known as a Yarn Needle or Darning Needle)

Yarn, yarn, yarn!

First and foremost, Crochet is a thread art, so you'll need yarn! The thread is used to make your project's cloth. It can be anything, from a garment to a home decor piece to a hubby toy for your children.

The weight and fiber contained in the yarn are used to classify it. There are a plethora of various yarn fibers to choose from. Polyester, acrylic, linen, superwash merino, cotton, and a variety of other materials are among the most popular.

There are also seven different weight categories. Lace (zero), superfine (one), fine (two), DK/light (three), medium (four), bulky (five), super-dense (six), and jumbo (seven) are the different types of yarn available.

Chunky yarn is one of the favorites since it knits together easily and, of course, makes super soft blankets. Consider using a medium to heavy yarn when you're first starting out. It's inexpensive and easy to use!

Crochet Hooks

Have you ever mixed up knit and Crochet? Let me clear it up for you because a great many people do!

Knitting and Crochet are distinguished from the usage of two pointed needles in knitting. You do need one curved hook to Crochet.

Hooks come in a variety of shapes and sizes. Aluminum, bamboo, ergonomics, rubber, and handcrafted are only a few examples.

I have a variety in hooks of various sizes, shapes, and labels. I began with a full beginner's range and then experimented with various styles here and there. You'll discover which hooks you prefer for which tasks when crocheting.

Simply make sure the hook size suits the recommended size upon the yarn label when purchasing a hook for a specific yarn.

Ergonomic Hooks

Ergonomic hooks normally have a kind of hold on the handles so that the hand is less stressed when crocheting. I've never known why anyone needs an ergonomic hook when every hook used in the past have served well. If you have problems with your wrists and hands being sore or cramping quickly then use clover crochet hooks.

Aluminum & Plastic Hooks

Plastic and Aluminum hooks are inexpensive and available in a variety of sizes. Both are fantastic! Since the rubber hooks are flimsy, they find it a bit more difficult to operate the stitches. They could even crack; aside from that, they're pretty nice!

Tapestry Needle

A tapestry needle is an essential component of your simple crochet supplies. It resembles a sewing needle, but it has a softer tip to avoid pricking you or splitting the thread. Until you've finished and tied off your project, they are used to weave in the sections of your yarn.

You may even use this needle to stitch the job together. For instance, whether you're crocheting granny square blankets or a variety of other crochet garments.

Tapestry needles with a bent tip are even better, particularly when sewing amigurumi together. They remind me of the tapestry needles' ergonomic hooks.

Hook Case

This is an optional item, but you would most likely need a case or, at the very least, a place to store your crochet supplies. You're ready to go if you have a cabinet or a drawer set aside exclusively for Crochet. If you need a case to hold things together, go to the nearest art shop, which is the expert's personal preference.

Stitch Markers

Stitch markers aren't absolutely required when you're first starting out, and not every pattern needs them. However, it's for sure that you'll wish you had such a package of stitch markers at any stage during your crochet adventure.

Stitch markers may be used in a variety of ways, including:

• If you're crocheting a big project, stitch markers will help you maintain track of the rows, so you don't lose track.

• Stitch markers are used to point out the first stitch of each round while crocheting in the round. This is advantageous when making amigurumi.

• Stitch markers come in handy while making a dress, particularly for labeling armholes and holding panels together when stitching.

• Plus, there is a slew of other options that you'll discover.!

Tools to make Crochet easy to use

1. Ergonomic Hooks:

Crochet is a new activity for you, and you're always learning how to do it, so it is understandable if you don't want to invest the extra money on those ergonomic hooks. But hooks that are ergonomically designed provide very nice grip and are very easy to handle.

2. Ball Winder:

Store-bought skins are transformed into tiny yarn cakes with this convenient ball winder! They're adorable, and they make things easy to fit yarn cake into a yarn bowl

1.3 Basic Crochet Stitches and Patterns

Crochet is a simple craft to pick up. To start making a wide range of designs, you just need to recognize some stitches. This guide includes tutorials, animations, useful hints, and some ideas related to the project for the six most traditional novice crochet stitches.

You'll be able to create a slip stitch and a crochet chain in no time, allowing you to begin simple crafts. Learn simpler stitching after that and start making scarves, and coats.

1. Crocheted chained stitches

Learn the slip knot before moving on to the chain stitch because it's what you'll need to obtain the thread/thread on the hook so you can start crocheting. The chain stitch, also known as the base chain, foundation chain or starting chain, is used to start most crochet projects.

Crochet links, particularly while doing some work in the circle, are often used to bind multiple stitches in some kind of a crochet pattern.

Picot stitches are typical Crochet edging with a texture created by a crochet cord. Crocheted chain are a popular design element in mesh or openwork lace o, wide loops.

Experiment with a plain crochet chain in some easy projects. Create the first easy crochet scarf by crocheting a pair of beautiful chain and knotting them around both sides.

2.Crochet Slip Stitches

Slip stitches in Crochet are tiny and plain. All Crochet is built on top of them. In designs slip stitch is commonly abbreviated as "sl st." When operating in the circle, the slip stitches are more often seen when you're told to "slip stitches to close round" or "enter with slip stitches to shape a ring."

Slip stitches may be used to connect two crocheted elements. Position some granny square beside each other and slide bring them together, for example;

Crochet slip stitch is often used to apply flourishes to projects. Slip stitches, for example, bring it to appeal to the upper layer stitching pattern in surface crochet. It's almost as though you're embroidering a masterpiece on piece with slip stitching.

3. Single Crochet Stitch

The crochet chain with slip stitch provides a strong base for beginning crochet projects. Each crochet stitch allows you to crochet a wider range of projects. The particular crochet stitch, abbreviated as "sc," is seen in several designs. The particular stitches are small stitches that work together to make a thick yarn. You may produce different densities by using different sizes of hooks or threads, as well as changing the thread. You will customize each stitch based on which loops you operate along until you've mastered it.

In all amigurumi crochet designs, the single crochet thread serves as the base stitch. Knitting or crocheting little plush dolls and other three-dimensional objects is known as amigurumi in Japan. Crocheting gives amigurumi pieces the perfect density of cloth.

4. Half Double Crochet Stitch

The half double crochet stitches add an additional step to the simple single crochet stitch. Half double crochet stitches have a height that is midway between double crochet stitch and single crochet stitch, and Most designs use the stitch, which is abbreviated to "hdc. The half double crochet stitches are a bit more open as compare to the single crochet stitches, yet it still provides adequate density for warm crafts. Half double crochet stitches are often faster as compare to single crochet stitch at creating cloth. When you need to knit a project quickly, this stitch comes in handy.

5. Double Crochet Stitches

The double crochet stitches (abbreviated "dc") works along with many of the other simple stitches. Granny square Crochet, fillet crochet, v-stitch Crochet, and other traditional crochet designs all use the double crochet stitch. Basic double crochet stitches are used in these patterns to give an otherwise simple project a new look.

You can make the double crochet stitches appear different based on which loop you work through until you've mastered it. Continuing to work in the back loop, for example, results in a ribbed pattern that looks great on blankets, cuffs, and hatbands.

6. Treble Crochet Stitch

In crochet designs, the treble crochet stitch, sometimes identified as the triple or trio crochet stitches, is shortened as "tr." The threads are taller than the double crochet stitches and have the same simple measures as the double crochet stitch.

You will create several various kinds of longer crochet stitches until you learn how to double the Crochet, like double treble and triple treble are much taller stitches. This stitch may be used to easily increase the height of a project. Longer stitching results in a looser thread. Crochet fabric that is looser drapes smoother and absorbs more, making it suitable for free, lacy garments and light blankets with tall stitches.

You're well on the way to being an expert crocheter now that you've mastered these six simple crochet stitches. Experiment with new stitch designs by mixing simple crochet stitches. The crochet seed stitch, for example, alternates single and double crochet stitches, while the crochet moss stitch alternates single and double crochet stitches. You'll quickly be able to confidently pick up some novice crochet designs.

Chapter 2: Crochet Clothes and Accessories Projects

Why do we like crocheting so much? It's breathable, light, and sultry, and it'll go with all of your summer basics. This knitwear is an excellent way to add a touch of femininity and warmth to your outfit. Since this fabric is influenced by the 1970s, you must wear it correctly;

otherwise, you may seem to be a grandmother. Don't worry; several designers have used this fabric in their contemporary collections. There are many lovely ways to wear Crochet though remaining contemporary. This delicate fabric goes with everything. See-through crochet tops look great with micro, sketch, and full dresses. Since this fabric draws eyes from the first glance, you can hold your accessories to a minimum.

2.1 Crochet Crop Top

Crocheted crop top is a must-have accessory for your summer wardrobe. Create one's own crop top using a trendy halter neckline instead of looking all over for one you like. The top slips together easily when you're knitting a single item that covers front of your chest while keeping the back exposed. You'll just only need a skein of yarn, a few simple crocheting abilities, and around 20 minutes to complete this project.

Do you aspire for high-fashion and chic looks on a daily basis? We've got a crochet top design for you that will make a huge style statement in your summer and spring wardrobes! This exclusive piece we're talking about is crochet tops, which will brighten the day by draping themselves over you as a light yet trendy layer of clothing! This series of 60 free crochet summer tops patterns are all simple to Crochet and suitable for intermediate to beginner crocheters!

These exclusive crochet patterns will add a pop of color to your spring and summer wardrobes! This would be a great way for you to show off your crochet skills.

2.2 Open Crochet Sweater

Cardigans are usually open fronted with buttons or zippers; robs, on the other hand, are bound dresses. The dress hangs open by nature and has no buttons or zippers as part of a new fashion pattern. A pullover (or sweater), on the other hand, would not expand in the front and maybe be pulled over the head in order to be worn. It can be knitted by computer or by hand. Cardigans were traditionally made of linen, but they may now be produced of cotton, synthetic fabrics, or a mixture of the two.

Simple cardigans are sometimes used over shirts and within suit jackets as an alternative to the waistcoat or vest that keeps the necktie in place when the jacket is removed. Its flexibility allows it to be worn in both casual and formal environments, as well as in every season, though it is most common in the fall and winter.

Monochromatic cardigans, whether long or short-sleeved, may be considered a conservative fashion classic. It is worn over a button-down dress shirt as a piece of formal wear for both men and women. Wearing a T-shirt underneath is a less formal choice.

2.3 Crochet clutch bags

Every woman's bag and purse is an important accessory that she likes to wear anytime she leaves the house. Suppose she is just visiting a place or going shopping. In the store, there are many lovely and charming purses and clutches to choose from. Because, like all other items, they are costly, and women must pay a high price for them. However, if you are skilled at crocheting and enjoy making stuff with your hands, you would have no trouble finding a lovely and adorable clutch bag without breaking the bank. Crocheting isn't just about wearing accessories; it's expanded to include a whole range of applications and possibilities. Lady's clutch packs, like many other items, maybe crocheted. There are some very important clutch bag designs that all of you must research about.

Uses:

A clutch is a lightweight handbag that can be kept in your hand or under your arm. The Clutch is a small bag with no belts or handles that are often used for evening occasions to hold minimal necessities such as a laptop, credit cards, or cosmetics.

Five Most Used Crocheted clutch bag patterns:

Many of the crochet clutch bag-free designs are a combination of basic and intermediate crochet stitches. And I have provided you the full guide for each. Many lovely and bold to light colors have been included in the crochet clutch bag-free designs available on different sites on the internet. But if you'd like to incorporate some other color, you can adjust the yarn's color to offer them a special touch. The fascinating thing about clutches is that you can avail stunning and fun clutch bags without wasting a penny on the market. Moreover, they are unique for winters, but they would still be useable in summers also. You have to choose the yarn and crocheting hooks of your own choosing to get underway.

Chroma Crochet Bag

There isn't a single lady who doesn't like car-

rying a bag or wallet. It is regarded as an important accessory that a woman enjoys wearing anytime she goes shopping, on a picnic, to the office, or somewhere else. Purses and clutches come in a wide variety of styles and colors. A customized purse or wallet, on the other hand, has its own location and significance for a woman; additionally, like many other items, she must pay a significant amount of money to acquire it. And it's not uncommon for her to be unable to locate a suitable match or one that meets her preferences. This Chroma Crochet bag is ideal for women.

Crochet Mini Clutch Purse

Use this versatile mini bag also as a Clutch, pocket, or organizer for your purse or luggage—made it's of grey and blue cotton with a beautiful golden button and a vibrant blue paisley lining. Computer, keys, credit card, makeup, and cash are all easily accessible. When you don't want to wear a large pack, this is ideal. In your suitcase or suitcase, organize your necklace, hairpieces, and lipstick. It's small enough to go in your bag.

Crochet Clutch Wallet

This crochet purse is more than that. Is it a pencil case? The scale is ideal. If you have a cosmetics bag? Well, absolutely! Is there a purse organizer? It's fantastic! For a night out, how about an actual handbag? Yes, yes, yes, yes, yes, yes, yes, yes, yes, yes. What's the difference between a book cover, a notebook cover, and an e-reader cover? Test, check and check again. Create a pair of extra Crochet clutches to give away, whatever you plan to use it for. Imagine a woman older than the age of 12 who does not enjoy such a unique, thoughtful, and realistic homemade gift this holiday season.

Crochet Perfect Purse

Prepare for the summers with this Stylish Purse Free Crochet Pattern, which will add a splash of color to every summer ensemble.

It's the perfect size for holding the necessities. It allows you to quickly stash your

pocket, tablet, and other loose objects. Single Crochet is used by the body. The lace design is seen on the top surface of the purse. The purse fills up quickly.

Crochet Puff Clutch

We guarantee you'll be fending off praises once you pull out this Clutch, which uses a puff stitch method to bring texture and interest to the crocheted cloth. The main part of the bag is made of mustard yellow yarn with a fluorescent pink tassel, but you can choose whatever paint you choose. Only make it clear that you have sufficient yarn before you start – although puff stitch seems to be a small project, it takes a tonne of yarn and tension may differ greatly. When making the stitches, try to make each loop as even as possible, as this would guarantee that the actual puffs are the same size.

2.4 Crochet Arm Bracelet

Crochet bracelets have so many benefits that we can't keep track of them all. For starters, they're fast projects that provide immediate gratification. They don't need a lot of wool, and you can make them out of normal yarn, crochet thread, or wire. They're ideal for putting a new methodology to the test. They will make exquisitely lovely presents for people of all ages. Beads, ribbons, charms, and buttons are all possibilities (or keep it simple and smooth with no added features). The list continues on and on. To enjoy all of the perks, try one of these beautiful crochet bracelet styles.

Corset Cuff Crochet Bracelet

This stocky crochet bracelet has a sexy look and finishes with a ribbon crop top strap, making it simple to find the perfect fit. The chunky cuff is made with plain crochet stitches and beads for a more advanced look with a bohemian flair.

lry.

Quartet Sugar Skull Bracelet

This vibrant crochet bracelet is ideal for a day of the Dead or other amazing events like the Halloween celebrations, but it can also be worn year-round as a statement item. It's made of weight yarn and has little buttons for closure.

Beaded Pop Tab Bracelet

With some quick crochet and a few little beads, you can make a fantastic upcycled crochet bracelet out of your pop tabs from any old soda cans. Half double and Single crochet stitches are used in this crochet design.

Beads & Fringe Bracelet

This lovely lace bracelet is the perfect addition to every woman's wardrobe. Delicate beads are encased in flouncy Crochet and tied together with a beautiful ribbon tie.

Free Form Bracelet

As you practice the technique of freeform Crochet, learn how to customize this simple crochet bracelet design using your own imagination. Keep it a solid color or make it much more vivid, depending on your preferences.

Crocheted Wire Bracelet

Take the existing crochet abilities and add them to your working with the thread. Just a simple crochet stitch and a desire to work with beads and wire are needed for this crochet design.

Leah Bracelet

Small chains loop around your wrist to create a fragile bracelet with plenty of effects. To create

this delicate accessory, you'll need a tiny crochet needle and crochet thread.

2.5 Crochet Ribbon Necklace

Jewelry will brighten up any outfit, and it doesn't need to be made of precious stones, silver or gold. Not the true ones, at least. Crochet a brace of ribbon thread. And if you've never crocheted before, a ribbon yarn necklace is simple to create since the only stitch used is the basic one. Use pretty ribbon yarn to crochet this basic 5-strand necklace. Beads are knitted in when you go through each strand. The elegance of the ribbon threads, along with the elegance of the beads, makes a luxurious necklace.

Tips and customizing

When crocheting with any ribbon thread, bear in mind that it has a tendency to spin and curl when you deal with it. Though it can take some time to get used to, the culminating look of the chain will give the necklace threads an interesting, puffy appearance. Check out the list below for further troubleshooting and customization suggestions.

• Apart from the flexible closure, you will change the tailor the length of the chain strands to lengthen or shorten your necklace.

• To create a necklace of graduated length strands, make each one 1"-2" longer as compared to the one before it.

• Adjust the scale of the chain stitches by using larger or smaller hooks.

• If you're having difficulty threading beads through ribbon yarn, try using a matching color of crochet string. Make a beaded strand with the thread and attach them to the ribbon strands while putting together your necklace.

• Threading the thread through the beads may also be done using a large-eyed hook. If you don't have a needle, dab a tiny amount of craft glue on the end of the thread and curl it into a point. Allow the adhesive or glue to dry completely before using its tip like a needle. When you're done, cut off the glued tip.

• Add bulkier ribbon or strands to thread for a fuller brace.

Ribbon Yarn and Sources

Ribbon yarn with small panels suspended within rows of matching thread is often referred to as "ladder" or "trellis." It's a trendy yarn that looks and feels like gossamer art ribbon and is available in a range of fibers. Any ribbon yarns are produced with a single dye, and many are made with a variety of complementary colors. Ribbon yarns with matte and shiny bands, as well as yarn with a membrane

texture interspersed with strong woven areas, are available.

Ribbon yarn is normally only sold in limited amounts, and it is typically costlier than most forms of yarn used during crocheting or spinning since it is a popular yarn. Ribbon yarn is used in hobby stores and specialist yarn shops. For your ribbon thread needs, there are a plethora of online options. These yarns might or may not have gauges, but the gauge isn't necessary when making crochet ribbon necklaces, and the overall structure can be easily changed.

Although the initial investment of ribbon yarn can be prohibitive, necklaces produced from the yarn will quickly recoup the investment and generate a profit if sold.

Chapter 3: Crochet Kitchen and House Projects

Colorful Crochet may be used to decorate the whole kitchen. Crochet dishcloths can be used for the sink, countertop trivets, tablecloths, and more can all be made from these designs. With these versatile and amazing crochet designs for kitchens, you can add rich color and texture to any part of the room. For these designs, do use kitchen crochet or any other appropriate thread.

Famous Crochet Kitchen Patterns

Crochet Placemat Pattern with Matching Coasters

This coordinating collection of crochet coasters and crochet placements can brighten up your kitchen table. To produce luscious texture, this design utilizes double Crochet and single Crochet and tactical spacing. You shouldn't be shocked if your dinner guests pass their hands through the cotton under their cups and bowls.

Coaster

Of course, if you have 10m of various colors of identical yarns, you still have more options with a 5m of teal, 4mm hook, 10m of cream, DK (light worsted weight). Cotton yarn was used to make this basic coaster. Reverse dc edging, also known as crab stitch, is the secret to having a basic project like this appear tidy and

done.

Easy Free Crochet Placemat pattern

To build a new atmosphere around the kitchen table, you might want to switch out your placemats on a regular basis. Here's another placemat crochet template for you to use. This one is crocheted in half double stitch and finished with lovely scalloped Crochet edging.

Upcycled Crochet Scrubbies Free Pattern

This crochet tutorial will show you how to up-cycle mesh net produce bags. To render a scrubby with enough quality to make your pans and pots

To acquire sufficient quality to make your pans and pots in the bathroom, you can never get so many crochet scrubbies.

Crochet Kitchen Towel Pattern

Crocheted kitchen towels are also a must-have. You should have one on hand if you make a mistake or need to wash your hands. Some have very lovely stitch designs that work in such a way that the rows of color alternate without needing to swap colors per row. It's an interesting strategy that's well worth knowing.

Tulip Inspired Potholders Crochet Pattern

Beautiful crochet potholders may be used to cover a whole wall. They create a dazzling presentation that will bring joy to the faces of those who visit your kitchen. This style is perfect for spring, but the tulip design is subtle enough that you might have these in your kitchen throughout the year.

Retro-Modern Crochet Potholers

Here's another crochet potholder design for you to try out. Easy double Crochet and single crochet stitches and can be used to produce a wave ripple through the dishcloth.

The graphic and minimalist design fits well in futuristic kitchens, but it still has a touch of vintage charm that makes it suitable for country classic homes.

Waterlily Hot Pad Free Crochet Pattern

You might put your hot spots on a placements or crochet dishcloth or, but a crocheted trivet or hot pad is even cooler. This is a dense, double-thick crochet hot plate. Develop a beautiful flower pattern in the middle of this piece with textured stitching. It'll look amazing gracing your kitchen wall while it's not in use on your countertop.

Pan Handle Crochet Cozies

Do you have some hot pans in your house that are scalding hot to the touch? If that's the case, these crochet cosines can do the trick. That way, you won't have to use a potholder to reach the cast iron skillets when you're cooking. This is a basic template, but it's incredibly clever.

Crochet Oven Mitt Free Pattern

If you prefer a more conventional oven mitt for handling hot pans, you can crochet one. This is a simple free crochet design that is made up of semi-circles. It's shaped as a mini-mitt that covers your hand up to the elbow, but it can easily be made into a bigger mitt.

Burlap and Lace Crochet Silverware Pockets

These crochet silverware pockets, built to look like they're made of burlap and lace, can add rustic charm to your kitchen table. You might even pack these to go on a picnic with you. There are several crochet kitchen patterns available, but this one is completely exclusive.

Crochet Chair Socks

If you're using dining table chairs rather than, or in addition to, kitchen bar stools, make sure to crochet them as well. These plain chair socks are worn over the chair's thighs. It isn't to wake them up; it's to keep them from rolling around on the kitchen floor. It also gives the space a splash of color and a sense of humor.

Crochet Teapot Cozy Free Pattern

Many households have teapots in their kitchens. In such kitchens, the crochet teapot cozy is a must-have. Their design is simple and solid in color, making it suitable for any home.

Embroidered Crochet Teapot Handle Cozy

You don't really have to knit all the way through your teapot. Instead, just cover the handle with an eye-catching embroidered cozy. When pouring your tea, it will keep your hands clean. It will also keep your kitchen looking good.

French Press Cozy Free Crochet Pattern

If you prefer coffee to tea, you really should have a French in your house. Attach a buttoned-up crochet jumper to it to make it cozier.

Crochet Mug Cozy Free Pattern

You already have a tonne of mugs in your home (kitchen) if you're a coffee drinker. Put cosines on them all and pick the one that best fits your mood on every given day. On a rainy day, this rainbow style is ideal.

Kitchen Stool Cover Crochet Pattern

In your kitchen, do you possess bar stools? Crochet a blanket over them. It provides a cushioned feel to the bench, making it more natural. It also adds to the decor. T-shirt yarn was used to make this one.

Doily Stool Cover Free Crochet Pattern

Crochet is also a great way to dress up your kitchen bar stools. While this style resembles a vintage doily, it has been redesigned for more modern kitchens. You may also make similar doilies to be used as placemats using the key portion of the pattern. Buying this will never make you feel regretful.

Crochet Rag Rug from upcycled Denim

When crocheting your kitchen, don't worry about the tiles. A mat next to the sink is a great place to put your sense of color all the way down to your toes. This one-of-a-kind style demonstrates how to upcycle old Denim with

Crochet. It's a unique take on the classic rag rug.

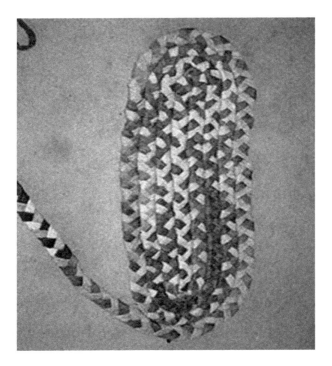

Crochet Hand Towel Free Pattern:

Crocheted kitchen towels are also a must-have. You should have one on hand if you make a mistake or need to wash your hands. Some have lovely stitch designs that work in such a way that the rows of color alternate without needing to swap colors per row. It's an interesting strategy that's well worth knowing.

Another free crochet design for a kitchen towel can be found here. This project is the ideal size for learning new stitches. The pique stitch is used in this one. To make a pattern that suits your kitchen decor, add paint stripes.

Spikes and Stripes Crochet Potholder Free Pattern:

Another great kitchen idea is crocheted potholders. They may be used to remove hot pans from the stove or to position dishes for serving. These potholders are thick, durable, and well-made. They're meant to be included, not just for decoration, though they do look nice. You'll mainly use simple crochet stitches, although the double-stitched spike stitch can be included for additional style information.

3.1 Crochet Placemats and Coasters

This light and lovely crochet placemats design are ideal for every season and time of year! You should offer them to your family members as gifts, and they are of an excellent standard and can be appreciated by everyone. This is due to the fact that everybody has a dining table and everybody enjoys making their home look nice. You may find these trends are difficult to follow but don't worry! If you know a few simple crochet stitches, such as half double and single, double Crochet, they'll be a breeze.

Crochet Placemats Pattern

These light and lovely crochet placemats designs are ideal for every season and time of year! You should offer them to your dear ones as gifts, and they are of an excellent standard and can be appreciated by everyone. This is due to the fact that everybody purchases a dining table and everybody enjoys making their home look nice. You may find these trends are difficult to follow but don't worry! If you know a few simple crochet stitches, such as half double and single, double Crochet, they'll be a breeze. Making new crochet placemats for each season or occasion is a perfect way to put these crochet placemat designs to good use. For Christmas, you should render red and white ones, and for Halloween, orange and black ones, and so on! This book would go over a variety of crochet placemats, ranging from oval to rectangular, doily to the mandala, American flag to colorful chevron designs.

Crochet Oval Placemat & Coaster

That's a lovely placemat you've got there. It's a cream and greyish-brown paint mix! Isn't that incredible? It will give your dining room a royal feel when you put it on the table! Start with 19 stitches chained together and move up. This project seems to be difficult, but all you really need are a few simple stitches to complete it!

• Bernat Handicrafter (290 yards for the primary paint, 145 yards for the opposing color)

Crochet Placemat Pattern

All adores and appreciates a one-of-a-kind pattern with a variety of lovely colors. It's really simple to learn and recreate. What you need are a few simple stitches and looping techniques. The end result is simply beautiful, and it will be the ideal way to get some color and comfort into your home! Since they're heavy and dense, they're ideal for creating during the fall season.

• Crochet hook, size G, 4mm

• Yarn Weight: Sugar Wheel Cotton Yarn Bee (1 skein at placement)

• Finished Dimensions: 18" width and 12" tall.

Crochet Placemat

Mandala designs are incredibly elegant and royal. They give any home, in any corner, a great vibe! This is due to the exquisite detail in its design as well as its lovely form. You'll need to know how to crochet half double, double, single crochet stitches. You'll still need to be familiar with a few more advanced stitches, such as and two double cluster crochet, spike double, and treble.

• Crochet hook size: 5mm

• Yarn: 3.5 lb., five shades, acrylic (14" – 16" diameter)

• 11" Finished Size.

Crochet Jute Placemats Pattern

Making these crochet placemat designs is a lot of fun! If you know what made the ideal pairing? This lovely pattern can be produced by combining two simple styles: rustic and trendy! Doesn't it sound wonderful? It will send off a clean vibe, while rustic will give it a unique look. Making a beautiful magic ring is the first step in this mission. It will aid in the creation of a far more stable finished product.

• Crochet Hook Size: 10mm

• Weight of yarn: 3-ply jute rope (65 yards)

• Dimensions: 12 in. diameter.

Round Placemat Crochet Pattern

These are so easy to bring for your dining table that all you need. It may be challenging to obtain this flat outcome if you use a lot of knots, so be patient and observe the measures carefully. Put this on the dinner table to make it more interesting, as well as to liven up your lunch during dinner breaks! It will brighten the day if you do see it every morning!

- Thickness of thread: 2.5 ounces or cotton yarn

- Thread will be 2.5 ounces in weight, and cotton wool will be used.

- 13" x 13" Finished Dimensions

Crochet Doily Placemat Mandala

If you want to make your house a little less depressing, what should you do? Using bright coolers will help you do this. The color scheme in this style is perfect for the job! Yellow is a happy, bright color, and blue has been scientifically shown to help you relax and feel better! Place these tiny mats on the dining table, which just need a few basic skills to create. You'll be happy with the outcome.

- Wool: sport weight, size 2

Crochet Placemats

Often what we want is something plain and straightforward. Anything that would not necessitate a lot of effort but nevertheless gets the job accomplished. Here's the ideal placemat, which can create in no time and even when enjoying a movie or television program. It's one of those crafts where all you have to do is repeat the same simple stitches over and over before you have the scale and proportions you like.

• Crochet Hook (size 9): 9.0mm

Free Crochet Farmhouse Placemat Pattern

What do you think about when you hear the words "rustic" and "yellow"? A farmhouse, indeed! You might want to make all of these and bring them with you on your next outing to the farmhouse. With these placemats, your food and meals can be very enjoyable and appropriate. Their vibrant coolers will bring a smile to everyone's face. Like the many other crochet placemat designs, this one is simple and quick to create, but you'll need to know how to use the TSC stitch.

- Worsted Weight Yarn

- Finished Dimensions: 13" x 19"

Bright Chevron Placemat

Crochet this Vibrant Chevron Placemat to match the summery vibes. These mats' vivid colors will add life to your home. You will feel revitalized any time you see them. You should knit all of the chairs in the same color or make your family members have their own colors. A multicolored placemat style is a novel and refreshing concept. Your table would undoubtedly be covered by the placemats.

- Lion Brand three hundred and twenty (320) yard yarn

- I/5.5mm hook scale

Easy to Crochet Plaid Placemats:

These placemats would go well with your home's classic and graceful theme. With their neutral and delicate colors, Plaid crochet placemats are simply beautiful. When placed on them, they can effortlessly make anything stand out. Stripes in various colors often liven up the bar. You should still go for a different paint scheme. To create these mats, you'll need a basic crochet kite and a lovely item to add to your already wonderful cooking. Tangerine, Ecru, Robin's warm brown yarn, egg and sage green: Lily Sugar's Cream, 100% cotton.

Tangerine, Ecru, Robin's warm brown yarn, egg and sage green: Lily Sugar's Cream, 100% cotton.

- I-9/5.5mm hook scale

- 18"*12" finished scale

Crochet Rectangle Placemat Patterns

This rectangular crochet placemat with soft hues and a perfectly patterned style is sure to please the minimalists that are out! The color scheme for this crochet placemat design is influenced by the Nordic theme. You'll only need two skeins of each color of yarn. Eight sets in 10 rows are the recommended gauge. By operating with a closer tension than most crochet materials, you will achieve a far more compact finish.

• Weight of yarn: (8 wpi)

• Hook diameter: 2.0 mm

• Yardage ranges from 327 to 328 yards.

Crochet Table Mat

Even just looking at color blocks is a joy! Do you like crocheting, color, and aesthetics? You've arrived at the ideal spot. Making these crazy fast peasy placemats would be a breeze. These are simple enough for even the most inexperienced to master. These placemats are 41 cm x 30.5 cm in size. The best thing about it? Crocheting each row will take you less than 5 minutes. Isn't that incredible? Go ahead and click the connection to get started.

• Hook: 2.5 • Hook: 2.5 mm

• Yarn: 8ply cotton mix

3.2 Crochet Twin Baskets

Crochet basket designs may be used to make one-of-a-kind storage solutions. They add character to your room and serve as attractive grab areas for your belongings. Crochet baskets may often be used as presents or for the holidays. This free basket design series has a wide range of uses, stitches, tools, and designs to make basket-making enjoyable!

Simple Crochet Basket: If you're searching for a quick and easy crochet basket, look no further than this tutorial. It employs common crochet stitches in varying heights that are simple enough for a novice to master. It has single Crochet edging on the back. The information is given to tightening the basket so that it can properly maintain its shape. The basket may then be embellished with bow and appliqués.

T-Shirt Yarn Crochet Nesting Basket:

T-shirt thread is among the strongest options for creating any size crochet container. The thick yarn, paired with the proper stitching, results in baskets that are durable and can hold straight up before caving in on the edges.

Yarn Stash Basket Crochet Pattern

What would you bring in your crocheted basket? If you're crocheted, you'll need it as a storage space for more yarn! This crochet basket design makes a huge basket that can carry all the yarn you'll need for a large project. This is also a perfect excuse to show off your yarn, and you'll get ideas for new designs.

Textured Crochet Basket Free Pattern

This big crochet basket pattern is also suitable for storing wool. It also fits with larger products like infant dolls or office supplies. This basket brings a splash of nice decoration to your home with its lovely textured stitching and fantastic colors. It's simple to bring from room to room, thanks to the built-in crochet handles.

Apple Basket Free Crochet Pattern

Give a neighbor, a parent, or your child's instructor an apple basket with a special touch of a durable crochet basket. This basket is flexible enough to be used as a holiday basket and fruit basket at any period of the year.

Spa Basket Free Crochet Pattern

To make a lovely spa basket, stock the rectangular knitting basket with scrubbies, lotions and soaps; it's the ideal Mother's Day, birthday, or "only because" present. This knitting basket is indeed a perfect way to organize your bathroom's miscellaneous items so that they don't appear cluttered.

Himalayan Basket Free Crochet Pattern

This crochet basket design has certain similarities to some of the other patterns on this page, but it uses special stitches that render it really unique. It's made out of t-shirt fabric and could double as a spa basket in bathroom storage. The twisted single stitch and spike stitch, on the other hand, really catch the eye in a different way. This basket is definitely a show-stopper!

Crochet Picnic Basket Pattern

Baskets are useful for storing items within the home, but they have been used to transport items outside. The outing basket is a classic case of two table basket. This basket pattern features a two-part lid which is reminiscent of picnic baskets. To intensify the impact, post stitches are used to produce a wicker-like texture.

Crochet Hanging Basket Pattern

You're not sure where you'll place more baskets in your home? If you can hold it up out to that way, it would improve. This encourages you to add a room to your home by only taking up a small amount of room. It's also a good way to get some color into your house.

Holiday Crochet Basket Patterns:

You might like a knitted basket for a special occasion. Knitted Easter Basket Designs like this one are common for giving homemade baskets to children who are heading for egg-hunting instead of store-bought ones. The same goes with Halloween trick-or-treating. Crochet Christmas boxes are perfect for making your own little gift packages. Make a holiday basket for every day!

3.3 Crochet Restroom Wipes

Crochet bathroom wipes are lovely crocheted fabrics that could be used for a variety of things, like covering toilet paper, soap, creating a cozy seat, and washing your hands. These toilet paper wipes are easy to clean and have a beautiful design. They are really affordable for the high quality they offer, so everybody can get their crocheted bathroom wipes from them and enjoy them!

Reusable Face Scrubbies

Crochet face scrubby is indeed a short and simple project that you'll enjoy making and gifting. They're reusable and washable, making them an excellent addition to the environmental skincare routine.

This beginner-friendly Crochet face scrubby design is simple to learn and fast to finish. You'll want to try out this template for the crochet cotton face scrubby if you need an easy present, a craft fair champion, or a little scrap-busting project.

Washable and Reusable

Crochet face scrubbies are reusable and eco-friendly, which is one of the aspects I like about them. Cotton rings or a face washcloth may be replaced by them. They're made of long-lasting cotton thread, meaning you'll be sure to wear them for a lot longer.

They're quite simple to maintain. Simply throw them in with the daily washing! In reality, with each wash, they'll get much softer.

Perfect for Scrap Busting

These scrubbers often don't need a tonne of yarn. A single skein of cotton fabric may be used to create up an entire stack of face scrub-bies! Alternatively, you should use whatever worsted weight weaved fabric you have on hand from previous designs.

A Great Crochet Gift Idea

A package of these handmade face scrubbies is a sweet gesture that can be given for a variety of reasons, including Mother's Day, a special holiday, Teacher Appreciation, or simply be-cause. Wrap a bar of cold and chilly around a rack of 5 scrubbies tied with a good ribbon.

Bath Pouf

This is a free crochet design for a bath puff. It's not as scratchy as a nylon pouf, but it also lathers up well with liquid moisturizer. This has a loop, so you can put it up to dry once you've used it. It turns out to be a good scale, measuring around 5 inches in its diameter. The best part about this design is that you create the hanging loop first, then the puff body. Many other designs need you to create the loop after the puff is completed because it's difficult to get inside the center of that same puff to fix it. And, despite the fact that it seems to be difficult to build the loop first then maneuver through it, it is not.

Soap Saver

Massage soap with the bumps and nubs on one side is lovely stuff. But what happens when you use soap? Within a few showers, those bumps are gone. What to do? Make the Pampering Massage Soap Saver! Many of these feature a lovely texture that makes them ideal for use as a washcloth as well. Simply put your soap into the soap bag and start scrubbing away. Then when done, simply hang them up to dry.

Washcloths

Here's a design that combines three different patterns into one! This is a fantastic concept for making three separate washcloths with matching colors. You might choose every paint scheme, and they'd all look great.

3.4 Crochet Cotton Ornament Flowers

With the holidays approaching, it's time to start bringing down the holiday decorations from the attic if you haven't already done so. Crochet Christmas ornaments are some of the most interesting (and adorable) holiday art projects you can make this time of year if you're like us and can't get enough of handmade decorations. Not only do those who look great on your mental or tree inside or out, but they're also a lot of fun to create. That's why we've gathered the following crochet designs, which range in difficulty from beginner to advanced.

Have your needles together because we've got knitting ideas that include everything from famous characters, including Santa and Rudolph, to cheerful classics like bulbs, bells and baubles. So, curl up on the sofa in front of a blazing fire, switch on your favorite Christmas or video, and begin crocheting. And there's nothing quite like crocheting to make you feel at ease, and few Christmas ornaments can mean as much to your family as ones you've created yourself. Check out some of our favorite crochet Christmas stocking designs when you're at it!

Here are some amazing crocheted cotton patterns:

Crochet a Beautiful Poinsettia Topiary

This potted topiary coated in crocheted poinsettias will add some positive vibes to your house.

Almost all adorable gets cuter when it's shrunk, which is surely true of such mini poinsettias. Working at this scale can be unfamiliar territory for you, but it's well worth the effort.

Create a Holiday Poinsettia Wreath

Adorn a wreath with crocheted poinsettias for a fun way to decorate this Christmas. Even if you live in a cold climate, you can hang this on your front door and not worry about the flowers wilting. Plus, it will last for years to come!

Tiny Crocheted Poinsettia Flower:

Almost all adorable gets cuter when it's shrunk, which is surely true of such mini poinsettias.

Working at this scale can be unfamiliar territory for you, but it's well worth the effort.

Make a Spiral Crocheted Christmas Flower

Even though the spiral flowers are not really meant to be poinsettias, the reddish one bears a striking similarity, and they make a perfect con-

temporary take on the traditional product. This sophisticated crochet design can be used wherever you choose to incorporate a seasonal motif. Scarves, placemats, and even a tea skirt come to mind.

Crochet Poinsettia in the Round

The sweet flowers will then be used to produce wreaths, gift sets, a wreath, and more.

Make a Snuggly Poinsettia Blanket

Are you ready to curl up in front of the fire or stream your favorite Christmas film? Crochet each square of these lap blankets with poinsettias! This pattern uses a grandma's square-like structure, so you can focus on the bits when you're out and about. Then, using single Crochet, connect the squares and attach a final edge.

Craft an Adorable Crochet Poinsettia

You'll create each petal, leaf and center separately for this poinsettia design before putting them together. This approach gives each item a special texture that sets it apart from the rest of the patterns on this chart. In addition, the free video demonstrates how to attach a felt backing to the pin and carry it as a pin.

Craft Poinsettia Gift Topper

These quick and easy crocheted poinsettias can add a personal touch to your presents. This project is simple and tactile, thanks to the bulky yarn. After unwrapping the package, recipients may attach a hanger to make it into an ornament.

Create a Dimensional Poinsettia Washcloth

With this washcloth, the bathroom gets into the holiday mood! This intermediate pattern, which features a 3D poinsettia in the middle, isn't the most practical, but it's adorable. You don't want to use a washcloth? Make a scarf out of a row of such squares!

3.5 Crochet Raffia Ornament Flower

Raffia is a fiber derived from the massive leaves of a palm tree stump native to Madagascar. Rayon raffia is used in these ornaments. Nashville Wraps is where you should have it. Raffia Ribbon is constructed of convenient rayon and comes in a variety of glossy pearlized shades on 100 yards rolls for beautiful gift wrapping. As a result, you should knit with raffia and use leftovers for packaging.

The leaves of a big palm tree may be removed and dried to make raffia strands. This natural fiber, like jute or cotton rope, maybe spun like straw, wrapped like silk sashes, or stuffed like foam. The grass-like material is common with milliners, craftsmen, and florists for a variety of tasks and gifts.

The creamy-brown sizes come from a particular palm tree that used to only grow on Madagascar's island. Raphia foraminifera has the biggest leaf of any tree stump, making it a natural fiber source. The fibrous leaves are sliced off and ripped apart in parallel lines, yielding very long strips of paper. In East Africa, the tree is now grown specifically for harvesting and sale.

Raffia is common with crafters because it is light, sturdy, and simple to dye. Cord, grass, leaves, silk, thread, padding, flower loop, and even paper may all be replaced with it. This natural material is used to make a number of caps, mats, baskets, belts, and twine. It's also used for applications in particular because it wouldn't shrink when wet but is still pliable enough to crochet. Raphia is produced from the leaf of the Raphia palm tree. It's available in both raw and dyed hanks from a number of retailers. Simple raffia work should be done by young children, who would be delighted with the attractive outcome. Certain methods require more experience and powerful fingertips, but it is essentially a simple art to master.

Decorative Stitching

Backgrounds for raffia sewing include canvas in both weights, Hardanger, and a burlap. They're all open woven, with evenly separated threads that can be numbered to ensure precise stitching. A huge fabric or knitter's needle is needed. Raffia may be used to create certain standard embroidery stitches on a wider scale. The following stitches are successful: running, skewing, satin, overhand, cover, tent, rug, stem, and herringbone. Raffia-stitched canvas may be used to create exclusive sheets, purses, and belts. **How to Make Crocheted Raffia ornament Flowers?**

All of the floral on this bright wall hanging was created using a plastic flower buckle. You may produce two sizes of raffia flowers with these looms: big ones on the external wires and tiny ones in the center. You may also mix the two to create a larger flower with a top-level of petals on the inside. With your loom, follow the directions to make four big, four double, and four tiny flowers in the color combination of your choice.

Assembling the Wall Hanging

On the 18-inch ends of the green burlap, turn in 12 inches. Hem or computer stitch is an option. Top and bottom, fold the rough edge under and turn in another 34 inches. Make a covering for the pieces of wood by stitching. Plan the arrangement on paper or lay the flowers out on the cardboard and transfer them about before you're happy with the outcome. Raffia is used to thread the tapestry needle, and large stem stitches are used to operate the stalks. If you like, you may combine two strands. Stitch the flowers in place from behind using an unseen thread across the centers. In the casings, position the dowel rods. Make a hanging cord out of a fine raffia braid and tie it to the top covering 3 inches from the foot. On the 18-inch ends of the green burlap, turn in 12 inches. Hem or computer stitch is an option. Top and bottom, fold the rough edge under and turn in another 34 inches. Make a covering for the pieces of wood by stitching. Plan the arrangement on paper or lay the flowers out on the cardboard and transfer them about before you're happy with the outcome. Raffia is used to thread the tapestry needle, and large stem stitches are used to operate the stalks. If you like, you may combine two strands. Stitch the flowers in place from behind using an unseen thread across the centers. In the casings, position the dowel rods. Make a hanging cord out of a fine raffia braid and tie it to the top covering 3 inches from the foot.

Conclusion

Crocheting and other methods of needlecraft or handicraft have been shown to have a variety of health effects, including tension and anxiety reduction. According to studies, the continuous repetition of hand movements tends to hold the mind relaxed and diverts the brain's attention away from life's pressures. The brain develops serotonin when crocheting, which tends to relax the mind and increase mood. Crocheting and other related behaviors have been found to help those with Alzheimer's, insomnia, and depression. The yarn's colors and textures are usually appealing to the eye, and the final product may provide a feeling of achievement.

Crocheting has been utilized by several primary school teachers to help their students improve their reading skills. Crocheting may aid in the development of fine motor skills in small children (such as handwriting). Crocheting in a literature environment helps young children to remain centered, multitask more effectively, and feel more enthusiastic about education. This enjoyable yet difficult ability will help students develop stronger interpersonal skills in their environment, with their classmates, and with their communities.

Knitting is easy, as you've probably learned. Crochet, on the other hand, is much simpler. If you've ever knitted before, crocheting is a breeze. Learning to Crochet is pleasant and rewarding, and with so many free crochet patterns online, getting started has never been simpler.

Two knitting needles are used while knitting. A single crochet needle is everything you need to start crocheting. Of course, you'll make errors at first, like in everything. Making small stuff like a lampshade, snood, or even a doily is a great way to learn what to do.

There are several guides accessible on the internet for studying various methods such as half double crochet, single Crochet, double bride, and magic circle and chain stitch.

Knitting is sometimes associated with tedious crafts because it is sometimes used as something to do in a care home. Knitting and knitting are closely linked, and a short web search can reveal just how many pleasant projects are accessible.

With the correct strategies and patterns, you will have fun right away.

Although Crochet, spinning, and sewing are typically associated with grandmothers, they may help you improve your dexterity. Crochet may help young people reduce their risk of arthritis and develop their fine motor skills. These precise motions necessitate hand mastery. In addition, you'll improve your hand-eye coordination.

Crochet will also help you improve your sense of contact. Doesn't it look nice to sit in a seat with a cup of coffee, your Crochet, and even a ball of wool? So let's get up and keep a pledge to yourself to learn to Crochet and show the world what you're capable of.

CPSIA information can be obtained
at www.ICGtesting.com
Printed in the USA
BVHW090059250521
607999BV00004B/841

9 781802 030051